THE
MEDICAL SCHOOL
INTERVIEW

*From preparation to thank you notes:
Empowering advice to help you succeed*

Jessica Freedman, MD

ISBN: 0615353916
ISBN-13: 9780615353913
Library of Congress Control Number: 2010922469
MedEdits Publishing
www.MedEdits.com

Author's note:

Some of the anecdotes I have used in this book are based on my actual experiences, but applicants' identities have been concealed. Some of this material, including the sample interview, is completely fictitious. Remember that plagiarism is illegal so do not regurgitate any of the information provided in this book for your actual interview or in your application materials. Authenticity is essential for your success so plagiarizing, even if you aren't "caught," will jeopardize your chances of admission. The information in this book does not guarantee that you will be accepted to medical school.

ABOUT THE AUTHOR

Jessica Freedman, MD is a former associate residency director and faculty member at the Mount Sinai School of Medicine in New York City. A top rated faculty member at Mount Sinai, she served on the medical school admissions committee and was involved in medical education and curriculum design at the graduate and undergraduate levels. She is also a published author and has served on national committees related to medical education. Dr. Freedman is now president of MedEdits, a private advising company for applicants to medical school, residency and fellowship. Dr. Freedman is a practicing emergency physician and lives in New Jersey.

TABLE OF CONTENTS

PART 1: ANATOMY OF THE MEDICAL SCHOOL INTERVIEW

PART 2: INTERVIEW PREPARATIONS AND FOLLOW UP

PART 3: SPECIFIC TYPES OF INTERVIEWS

APPENDICES

INTRODUCTION

I started my "interview career" as an interviewee myself when I was a premedical student and then again as a residency applicant, but I learned most about this process during the 10 years I spent in the interviewer's seat. Like most physicians, I had no formal training or experience when I started interviewing candidates. During my years of selecting candidates, I learned what qualities applicants must have to interview well. More important, however, I learned what goes on behind the scenes after interview day and how a candidate's success is affected by the interviewer's skills and experience. Indeed, I gained an understanding of how both experienced and inexperienced interviewers evaluate applicants and what applicants can do to influence these differences to their advantage. After working with applicants who are preparing for interviews with www.MedEdits. com, I also know what mistakes interviewees commonly make. These experiences, from both the "outside" and the "inside," allow me to provide a unique perspective to medical school applicants who are preparing for interviews. Thus, this book, based on my inside understanding of the medical admissions process and my work privately advising students, is a must-read for both interviewees and interviewers alike.* It covers everything you need to know, beginning with what you should do to prepare for interview day, what to expect on The Day, and the nitty gritty of how to behave during and after the interview. By having a full understanding of the medical school admissions process, knowing what goes on behind the scenes before and after your interview, who will be interviewing you, what the interviewer is looking for and what you can do to influence how your interview will progress, you will be better prepared to do well and present yourself in the best light.

*A NOTE FOR THE INTERVIEWER

I encourage medical school interviewers to read this book to gain some insight into how to make thorough, accurate and complete assessments of medical school applicants when you interview them. I find that many medical student interviewers and first time attending interviewers are often as nervous as the applicants! Based on my own experience in academic medicine, I know that we typically receive no training on how to interview applicants. In fact, I sometimes found myself teaching my senior attendings about how to review an application and interview an applicant to make sure all important information was obtained and to rule out any red flags.

There are always applicants who have "slipped through the cracks" when the admission committee failed to notice a significant piece of their history. These applicants may have difficulty in medical school or residency or as attendings, and it is therefore the interviewer's responsibility to make sure such individuals are identified. Failure to do so not only compromises a seat in a medical school or residency class when a student cannot complete a portion of his or her education but may also negatively affect patient care. I work primarily with applicants, but I have also helped friends and colleagues to refine and improve their interviewing and application reviewing skills.

CHAPTER 1

WHO GETS INVITED FOR AN INTERVIEW?

A wide range of people screen medical school applications and decide who should be invited for an interview, including current medical students, attending physicians, medical school administrators and basic scientists. Some schools and programs have minimum cutoffs for grades and standardized test scores, and the application of anyone who does not reach these levels does not even make it to the screening process. Some schools assign "points" for everything: extracurricular activities, medical college admissions test (MCAT) scores, and letters of recommendation; you are invited for an interview only when your score meets a minimum number. More often, whatever the grading system, a great deal of subjectivity goes into the decision to invite an applicant for an interview. Frequently, the screener's personal interests and outlook play a part in the review of your application--especially if you are a "borderline" applicant. For example, if reviewer A always had to struggle with standardized tests yet managed to succeed while reviewer B always had board scores in the top fifth percentile, reviewer A is much more likely than reviewer B to screen in an application with lower-than-average board scores.

The person reading your application might have years of admissions experience or he or she could be a novice, such as a medical student or a junior faculty member. Both the level of experience of the screener and his own biases and preferences often determine whether or not you are granted an interview. Also, although the person reading your application might have hours to peruse through all of your materials, it is more likely that she is tired and rushed and has a large pile of applications to review. If your application follows one that is more stellar, yours may pale in comparison. On the other hand, if the pile contains mostly mediocre-to-poor applications, yours may stand out.

For all of these reasons, making your application as distinctive as possible increases the likelihood you will be invited for an interview. If the application bores the person reading it, you will likely end up in the rejection pile. But you must also understand that many applicants to medical school are highly qualified and that many steps in the selection process are out of your control. This is a hard truth to accept, and you can only hope that your application and letters of reference are appealing enough to trigger some medical school interview invitations. Each interview is a chance for acceptance, so it is essential to be prepared and know what to expect.

CHAPTER 2

WHAT ARE THE DIFFERENT TYPES OF INTERVIEWS?

You typically will know in advance what type of interview each school conducts, which should help to prepare you psychologically and literally. Below are the five major types of interviews.

Open file

An open file interview is the most common type. In an open file interview, the interviewer has access to all of your information, including all written documents, letters of reference and test scores. But just because an interview is open file does not mean that the interviewer has read all of your materials. Your interview is just one part of his day, and if the interviewer was awakened at 2 AM for an emergency, he probably has not had time to read through your file. Or, maybe your interviewer was teaching a class that ran late, and he had only five minutes to review your materials. You must prepare for an open file interview in the same way you would for a closed file interview (discussed below). Do not assume that your interviewer knows a thing about you. Also, do not be offended if your interviewer reads your file while you are speaking. This may be the first time he has glimpsed your personal statement, application and letters of reference.

Closed file interview or partial file interview

In this type of interview, the interviewer may have no or limited access to your materials. These interviews therefore offer an opportunity to control the interview and dictate what is discussed.

Panel interview

Applicants tend to find a panel interview more intimidating than any other type. Typically, the panel comprises three interviewers and one interviewee. How this interview proceeds depends in part on the dynamic and hierarchy of the interviewers. For example, a junior faculty member may be intimidated by a more senior faculty member and therefore may be more concerned with her own performance than with the interviewee's. It is important during these interviews not to psychoanalyze the group who is interviewing you but to stay focused on their questions and your own personal agenda of what you hope to convey.

Group interview

These interviews typically involve several interviewers and interviewees. Their objective is to see how you manage pressure and how you respond to others. You should listen attentively to everyone's answers and be a team player. If someone gives an answer that you wanted to give, make a joke: "John just gave my answer and now I have nothing to say." Do not act as though the other interviewees are competitors. Listen respectfully to what they have to say, make eye contact and be interested in everyone. Though it is natural to compare yourself with other interviewees in the group, be aware that the other interviewees' answers may "sound better" than your own not because they actually are superior to your answers but because their stories are new to you.

Multiple mini interviews

This type of interview was developed in Canada, and only a few schools in the United States use it. Students rotate through a variety of "stations," remaining at each for eight to 10 minutes to address a particular question. For example, the interviewer may give you a scenario and ask how you would behave, how you might describe the situation to a person involved in the scenario or how you would interpret the issues the scenario presents. In general, these mini interviews are designed to evaluate your professionalism, communication skills, ability to work with a team, compassion and ability to consider all aspects of a situation. Since this type of interview is rare in the United States, this publication will not discuss it further.

CHAPTER 3

WHAT IS THE INTERVIEWER LOOKING FOR?

It is important to understand what interviewers are looking for within the context of your experience. Medical school applicants often fail to make a good impression when they try to tell interviewers what they think they want to hear instead of representing themselves honestly and authentically. Since your grades, MCAT scores and letters of reference will be used to evaluate your academic aptitude, interviewers are trying to assess something else-- if you are genuinely committed to a career in medicine and have an understanding of what it means to practice medicine, if you have compassion, empathy, and maturity, your intelligence and how good your interpersonal and communication skills are— among other attributes. (See Box 1: What qualities and characteristics do interviewers evaluate?) Interviewers also want to rule out any red flags, such as gaps in time on your record, many changes in careers or interests or any signs of personal instability.

Do you have a demonstrated commitment to and understanding of a career in medicine?

Interviewers are trying to assess first and foremost your motivation to pursue a career in medicine. They want to hear about when and why you want to practice medicine, and they want to know that your background justifies your claim that you want to practice medicine. They also want to know that you understand what you are getting yourself in to and that you understand the pros and cons of practicing medicine and have a realistic idea of the challenges you will face in medicine. This is why some interviewers ask about health care reform; they don't expect you to have an advanced degree in health policy, but they want to know that you at least have some idea of what the issues in health care are today.

Are you confident yet humble?

Even a hint of arrogance or self-righteousness might destroy your chances of acceptance. Humility is much preferred over self-centeredness and a fine line sometimes differentiates confidence from overconfidence. Be sure not to do anything that might suggest you are overconfident, for example by acting too informal or familiar, appearing too comfortable, dropping names or obviously promoting yourself. Let your accomplishments speak for themselves and hope that your letter writers wrote about your positive qualities and attributes.

Do you have what it takes to make it through medical school, residency training and a future medical career?

It takes a tremendous amount of dedication, resilience and perseverance not only to succeed in medical school but also to do well in residency training, which can be very rigorous. While interviewers will glean information about your strengths based on what is written in your letters of reference, they are also trying to assess these qualities during your interview. A medical education and career pose intellectual, emotional and physical challenges that a medical school applicant cannot appreciate. So, it is your interviewer's job to decide if you have the characteristics that make it likely you will be able to cope and succeed throughout your medical education.

Can you recognize your faults and admit when you are wrong?

No one expects you to be perfect. In fact, admissions committee members want to know that you can recognize your faults and that you can make improvements or modify your behaviors. For example, if you had an institutional action during college, admissions committee members want to see that you are remorseful and that you have learned and grown from the experience. They also want to know that you are aware of your limitations. An important part of being a great doctor is knowing when it is time to ask for help and to be aware of your own strengths, expertise and weaknesses.

Is everything consistent?

Interviewers also want to make sure that what you have written in your application and how you present yourself "match." Misrepresentation in either your application or your interview makes a negative impression. Consistency in your story is key, and interviewers will try to identify themes in your background and during your interview.

Are you smart and intellectually curious?

You also are being evaluated on your intelligence, intellectual curiosity and your ability to think logically and critically. While you won't be asked academic questions, a skilled interviewer can assess your abilities based on how you reason through the questions that are asked.

What is your demeanor and how do you communicate?

Medical school applicants are judged on whether they are articulate, poised, enthusiastic and mature, can manage difficult questions with ease and demonstrate empathy and compassion. The best applicants smile, make good eye contact and are

engaging, interesting and warm. Be sure you aren't swayed by a negative interviewer. You should greet even the grouchy interviewer happily and warmly and don't allow them to "bring you down." People with "sparkling personalities" always do better on interviews than their more sullen, stone faced or negative peers. Interviewees are also judged on their accomplishments, life experiences, ability to overcome obstacles and their suitability for a career in medicine. Since communication skills, great interpersonal skills and the ability to relate to people are necessary to practice medicine, you may be dinged if your interviewer thinks you have difficulty in these areas.

Are you culturally competent?

As our country becomes more diverse, physicians must be able to care for individuals of different cultures, religions, races and socioeconomic backgrounds. This does not mean that admissions committees want to know that you speak a second language; rather, they want to know that you have experience working with people who are different from you and that you are sensitive to the impact of these differences. Can you communicate with patients who have diverse backgrounds? Will you be understanding of how these differences affect patients' compliance and perception of disease, and will you consider a patient's home and community environment when designing your treatment plan?

How will you add to the medical school's community?

Your interviewer also will evaluate how you will add to the learning environment and the diversity of the medical school. With the recent emphasis on a holistic review of applicants, this definition of diversity is broad and relates not only to your cultural and racial background but also to your interests and experiences. Most medical school interviewers are open minded and thus hope to attract a broad range of students to their school who can make a valuable and meaningful contribution to the medical community.

Are you a good "fit" for the medical school?

Schools also are seeking out applicants who are the best fit for their school. For example, a smaller community-focused school may not be interested in the applicant with 10 original publications who wants to make research a part of her career. So, while one applicant may be the ideal student for one school, she may not be the best fit for another. You therefore should study each school's website before you interview to have a sense of what it values, its mission statement and what kind of students it is trying to attract. As already emphasized, who you are on interview day must match the person the admissions committee reads (or will read) about in your application, but you can often spin your experiences a bit to conform to their ideal student and applicant.

Do you have any red flags?

The two most obvious red flags are gaps in time of longer than three months when you cannot account for your activities or frequent jumps in career without any real explanation for these changes. Both of these factors suggest a lack of commitment or some possible underlying problem. Students who cannot communicate or are extremely nervous or anxious also raise concern. Interviewers are also trying to identify any major personality disorder or psychopathology that may hinder a candidate's ability not only to interact with patients and colleagues but the ability to get through medical school and residency. Other common "red flags" include a low grade or MCAT score, an institutional action or withdrawals from classes but, typically, if you were invited for an interview, these issues were not considered major. That said, you should be able to give explanations for the flaws in your application without making excuses.

Have you overcome any significant hardship or adversity?

Students who have overcome significant obstacles such as coming from an underserved area, having financial hardship or being the first in their family to go to college are typically evaluated within the context of this cohort of applicants. Since achieving success with few resources is a tremendous accomplishment, students who have overcome adversity are looked upon favorably because achieving under difficult circumstances requires perseverance, drive and a true commitment. Also, people who come from underserved areas are more likely to serve such communities in the future, which is why it is in society's best interest (and the medical school's) to attract such applicants.

What element of diversity do you contribute?

Medical schools now emphasize a holistic review of applicants so they have a broad definition of diversity as mentioned above. Admissions committees are looking for students with a diverse mix of experiences, backgrounds and perspectives. This does not mean that being a traditional student is a liability. In fact, being traditional (meaning that you haven't had a prior career or come from an underprivileged background) also has advantages because traditional applicants typically present no red flags and are highly motivated and directed. But the applicant who had a prior career or who is an immigrant, for example, also brings diversity to a medical school class. Medical schools also seek to enroll a diverse mix of students with varied backgrounds and interests.

Would the interviewers enjoy spending long periods of time with you?

Since your interviewers not only see you as a medical student candidate but also as a potential future colleague, they want to know that you are, bottom line, good company. So, you must convey that "having you around" would be comfortable and pleasant. This is why small talk matters during your interview day; interviewers want to know that you are personable.

Are you sexist or racist?

Any hint that you are biased, not open minded and not sensitive will make interviewers check the "rejection" box. I remember how one applicant, when speaking of caring for an inner city population, said, "I have concerns about taking care of people who are underserved. I have never worked with those types of people before." While this comment may have been innocent, it struck the interviewer the wrong way, and she rejected this applicant.

Box 1

WHAT QUALITIES AND CHARACTERISTICS DO INTERVIEWERS EVALUATE?

Commitment to medicine

Understanding of medicine

Motivation to pursue a career in medicine

Clinical exposure and experience (such as shadowing)

Intellectual abilities

Intellectual curiosity

Scholarly interests

Level of compassion

Level of empathy

Level of altruism

Maturity

Warmth

Professionalism

Cultural competence

Resilience and perseverance

Experience in research

Experience in teaching

Community service experience

Work with underserved populations

Leadership ability

Ability to think critically and analytically

Ability to communicate

Ability to listen

Ability to answer difficult questions

Ability to work as a member of a team

Personality and overall disposition

Reactions to situations (Do you ever become impatient or react impulsively?)

Values

Ability to overcome obstacles and cope with adversity

Achievements that make you stand out

Level of initiative

Red flags

CHAPTER 4

WHO WILL INTERVIEW YOU?

Most interviews are conversational and biographical. You may be interviewed by admissions deans and directors, administrators in the admissions office, clinical faculty (the MD type), basic science faculty (the PhD type) or medical students. Typically, you will have two interviews, each lasting 30 minutes.

Always remember that your interviewer is your advocate. She (or he) will "sell you" to the admissions committee. Remember your interviewer is human and, most of the time, is not trying to "get you." She wants to find out about you as a person and if you will be a good fit for the school.

Because your interviewer is the primary support for your candidacy it is essential to get on her good side. Whether she writes up reports or summaries about you or presents you verbally to a committee, your interviewer typically makes or breaks your acceptance. If she thinks highly of you, you're usually in, but if you don't make a good impression, she will not support you. Because you cannot control or predict who will interview you, it is important to have broad appeal as an interviewee and prepare yourself for multiple scenarios.

Considering my experience working with many interviewers and many applicants, I find that the types of interviewers fall into eight general categories, each of which calls for a different candidate approach (see Box 2: Types of interviewers). But to direct an interview to your advantage, you need to try early in the interview not only to get a fix on which type of interviewer you have but her perspective and level of experience, which also will affect how your interview progresses. Because most medical school interviewers receive no training in interviewing candidates they do not necessarily know how to evaluate you comprehensively and effectively, as do more experienced interviewers. Why is this important? Because these inexperienced interviewers (who are most likely to be certain of the types described in Box 2) tend to ask more questions and have a different approach than more seasoned interviewers.

Box 2

TYPES OF INTERVIEWERS

The Mentor

The mentor is the most common type of interviewer and represents the typical medical educator. These interviewers tend to conduct relaxed yet serious interviews and have a fair amount of experience doing them. Typically, the mentor will ask you basic questions about your background and motivations. These interviewers are confident in their abilities, are committed to medical education and have extensive experience working with students. They understand that the best way to gain the greatest understanding of your motivations, intelligence and character is if you feel comfortable. Their questions therefore tend to be basic and predictable. Fortunately, most medical school interviewers are mentors, and, in general, the interviews they conduct are "easy." Indeed, most candidates walk away from these interviews feeling confident and thinking, "That interviewer really liked me." But, it's important not to become too comfortable and informal during these interviews simply because you feel confident that you are making a good impression. Remember that while the interviewer is your advocate, he is not your friend.

The Professor

These interviewers can, based on appearance, seem to be the most intimidating when, in reality, they are usually great interviewers. They are very experienced, have worked in different settings, have interviewed many candidates, residents and attendings and have a vast amount of experience. They know what they are looking for and how to get the information they need and are typically efficient in seeking it out. Thus, your interview with the professor may veer off in another direction; you may start talking in depth about your research or your interest in philosophy or medical anthropology. Unlike the question shooter and the "inappropriate" interviewer (see below), however, the professor typically goes off on a tangent because he has effectively and efficiently assessed your candidacy and therefore has time to spare. He is confident in his abilities and is comfortable getting off topic. In some ways, the professor is the interviewer you want; he typically has a strong political voice on admissions committees, and if he supports your candidacy he can be a tremendous advocate. But, the reverse is also true; if he is not in favor of you, his opinion will also weigh heavily

The Question Shooter

This is most students' worst nightmare. This interviewer might ask you what three people you would like to invite to dinner and why. He may also ask you about your greatest strength and weakness or ask you a very unusual question. Typically, the question shooter is inexperienced and asks questions because, he fundamentally doesn't know how to interview. He thinks asking random questions is what he is supposed to do and isn't even sure of the answers he is hoping to hear or how to evaluate your response. In some ways, these are the toughest interviews because you can in no way rely on your interviewer to ask you about what you want to tell him. The best way to manage these interviewers is to try to guide the interview. Make segues. Bring up topics you hope to discuss. (How to guide your interview will be discussed again later on in this book.)

Some schools have a standard list of questions that they like interviewers to ask candidates. This type of question shooter cannot typically be swayed. It is best to try and answer these questions as fully as possible, but don't expect the interviewer to "take the bait" of your segues and direction.

The Inappropriate Interviewer

You are unlikely to have this type of interviewer because she usually doesn't last for long on admissions committees. Typically, an applicant complains and this interviewer is asked to leave the committee. You can spot an eccentric interviewer by the way she asks you sensitive or even illegal questions, often boring into the most sensitive topic in your background and delving into it. These interviewers are insensitive and think that by "digging" they will gain more information about your character or motivations. They may also ask you illegal questions about your personal family goals. Again, the best way to cope with these interviewers is to try and guide your interview and bring up topics you would like to discuss. When asked a question that you think may be illegal, such as a question about your sexuality, family plans or religion, it is best to answer vaguely and to try and change the topic. If you are really offended by an interviewer's questions, you should tell the dean of admissions about your experience and request another interview.

The Egomaniac

Ah, the egomaniacs. They are tough nuts to crack. They are generally young and inexperienced, and they are psyched to be in a position of power. They think they have your life in their hands, and they have told all of their friends that they are on the medical school admissions committee. They proclaim to all that they are important. In some ways, the egomaniac is the toughest interviewer to impress, and it is not unusual for the egomaniac to want to hear himself speak as much as he wants to hear you speak. You cannot rely on the egomaniac to ask you about factors that will be relevant to your candidacy so you must guide your interview, and be sure to impart the information that you know is important.

The Strong Silent Type

The strong silent type likes to listen. These interviewers may not like to ask too many questions. These types are rare since, those who are shy do not typically volunteer to be on admissions committees. These interviewers are most challenging for shy applicants, and I envision a very quick interview when they get together. Your major concern if you get a strong silent type is that he is unlikely to loudly advocate for you during a medical school admissions committee meeting, so you must hope that the school requires only a written evaluation.

The "Sure, I'll Do It" Type

The "sure, I'll do it" interviewer is the person who was asked by his chairperson to serve on the medical school admissions committee or was pulled in at the last minute when an interviewer was desperately needed. This interviewer is usually participating because he thinks he "should" and may have a relaxed attitude or he may be really annoyed because he had other plans for his day that has now been interrupted because of your interview. Regardless, It is unlikely that he is fully invested in the process. With the former, these interviews tend to be fairly relaxed and undirected but if you get someone who may be annoyed, he may take this out on you. The issue with the "sure I'll do it" interviewer is that you must provide him with the information that you know is important. These interviewers may not be the strongest advocates. Thus, it is important to arm them with information about you and your motivations that they otherwise might not ask about.

The Student Interviewer

Many medical schools encourage current medical students to interview prospective students. But, like their faculty counterparts on the admissions committee, medical students frequently get little or no training on how to interview applicants. When I was on faculty, I thought that having current medical students (and current residents for residency) interview candidates was a great idea since they could judge an applicant's fit for the school. Now that I am privy to hearing about these interviews from the applicant's perspective, however, I think students sometimes lack the experience to make such influential choices. Many applicants often tell me, "My interview with the student didn't go so well." I think student interviewers leave this impression because often they don't know what exactly they are seeking. They tend to like concrete answers and often ask many specific questions (like the Question Shooter). They sometimes can become too informal with applicants and end up discussing personal issues and topics that don't relate to the applicant's candidacy. I encourage applicants to approach the student interviewer with the understanding that these interviewers are young and often immature and may not have any experience. Applicants therefore should make sure to approach the student interviewer with a clear idea of their strengths and the aspects of the application that they would like to discuss.

CHAPTER 5

MAKING THE MOST OF
THE INTERVIEW

Whatever type of interviewers you have or their level of experience, you can maintain some control of what transpires. (Even the "question shooter," while difficult to manipulate, can be directed by your responses.) Give complete answers (as a rule, never answer with a "yes" or "no") and elaborate. Do not memorize your answers or deliver something "canned." Expect the unexpected. You should try not to ramble, say "um" or "like" too much, fidget in your seat or display nervous tics. Here are some other general guidelines for making the interview go as well as possible and to make sure that you convey everything that you think is important about your candidacy:

Be authentic
This may seem simple, but interviewees who are "comfortable in their own skin" stand out versus applicants who try to say what they think everyone wants to hear. Even if your interviewer isn't specifically evaluating you on your authenticity, an applicant who speaks the truth in his own words typically exudes confidence and professionalism. Sometimes the most distinctive applicants are those who are the most natural and possess a true sense of themselves.

Make a good first impression

Even if it is subconscious, your interviewer makes a judgment about you within the first five to 10 minutes of your interview. If the interviewer has a positive impression, this "halo effect" will affect everything you say. Similarly, an initial negative impression will also cast a shadow and it will be tough to redeem yourself. Making a good first impression is based not only on what you say but on your general demeanor. Are you professional, poised, energetic, positive and enthusiastic? The impression you convey in the first few minutes by your overall attitude, energy, tone of voice and expression will set the stage for everything that follows. Remember never to say anything negative during an interview about other schools or people, which may give a poor impression.

Even small talk at the appropriate time can have an important effect, either positive or negative. You might find yourself speaking with a member of the faculty or a current student who is not interviewing you before the school presentation, for example. If this person has a strong impression of you, whether positive or negative, she will likely express it when your candidacy is discussed.

Create your own agenda

By agenda, I mean an outline in your mind (you don't want to display a crib sheet) of the key things about you and your experiences that you would like to discuss. This is essential because you cannot rely on your interviewer to ask about everything you would like to discuss, even all of your key experiences; you must take responsibility for bringing them up even if you wrote about them in your application. Remember that even if an interview is open file, your interviewer may not have had the time to review your materials. Also, think about how your experiences and values are similar to the mission and philosophy of the school to which you are applying. Be sure to speak about your experiences in this context.

Make the interviewer's job easy

When I interviewed applicants, the most painful interviews made me feel that getting information from an applicant was "like pulling teeth." In contrast, the easiest interviews were with candidates who had a lot to say that was pertinent and important. These interviewees were obviously better prepared, which impressed me because it indicated that they were taking the interview seriously enough to practice. Even though I was never a "question shooter," the applicants who gave brief answers forced me to dip into my "interview questions bank" since they said so little. Ideally, you should make your interviewer's job easy by providing her with insights and anecdotes and making segues. You don't want to ramble, but as long as you stick to the agenda you've created, it's most likely that you will stick to pertinent topics while making things simpler for your interviewer.

Make segues and give complete answers

Again, this comes back to the idea that you are in control. Make segues to topics you would like to discuss. For example, if you are asked why you want to be a doctor, explain not only "why" but "when" and "what." Tell the interviewer when your interest started and what you have done to explore it. By the same token, if you are asked "what is your most valuable volunteer experience" tell the interviewer not only "what" and "when" but also "why" and "how" you became interested in this activity. If you practice doing this, your segues should become natural and conversational, and your interviewer will remain engaged in what you are saying. By making these references and elaborating, you will naturally inspire further discussion and create prompts for your interviewer.

Try your best to make your interview conversational

The more experienced interviewers will naturally try to make your interview conversational but, just like any conversation, your interview is a give and take so do your best to keep the flow going. At the same time, be sure that you keep an air of formality to your interview even if your interviewer becomes too informal. Also, try not to dwell too much on one topic or to get off topic. Unless the interviewer is a dean of admissions or someone who is very experienced and has already covered many of the basics of your experience and motivations, you should make it your job not to allow the interview to get off track. This usually is a risk only with an inexperienced interviewer.

Bring up "red flags"

Be sure to strategically bring up any possible "red flags," but don't dwell on them. Don't make excuses for any flaws in your application. Explain why they happened succinctly, and be straightforward and matter of fact. You may think that it would be ideal if the interviewer doesn't bring up a red flag in your application, such as gaps in time or a low MCAT score or grades. In reality, it is best if you have an opportunity to address these issues during the interview because they inevitably will come up in behind-the-scenes discussions about you and, if your interviewer is not armed with an explanation, he will not be in a position to defend you. This puts you at a disadvantage.

Keep in mind that your interviewer's attention span is short

Don't speak for longer than three minutes about any one topic unless you sense that your interviewer wants to hear more. Pay attention to body language and cues; do you sense that your interviewer wants to interrupt you and ask a question? Does he look bored--should you wrap up your answer and allow your interviewer to move you to another topic? Is he making eye contact and acting engaged in what you are saying? There are no absolute rules for how long you should speak; it all depends on the dynamics of your actual interview.

Interviewing the interviewer

Do not turn the interview around on your interviewer and start asking her questions about her career and motivations unless this happens naturally. This can be interpreted as disrespectful or make the interviewer "work" when your job is to make hers easy. On the other hand, if an interviewer mentions things about herself or if you share common career interests and goals, it is only natural to ask her questions. This not only demonstrates that you are curious, but it also shows that you have excellent interpersonal skills, both of which are essential to practicing medicine. As with other aspects of the interview, what you discuss should be guided by the individual interviewer and the rapport between the two of you rather than by any firm rules.

Most schools will not identify your interviewer in advance, and I discourage applicants from seeking out this information. Even if the school's policy is to notify applicants in advance about who will interview them, I don't recommend researching your interviewer. Not only are last minute changes common, but interviewers are not concerned about how much applicants know about them. They are more focused on what you know about their school.

Remember, you cannot be prepared for everything

During the first five to seven minutes of your interview you probably will feel anxious or ill at ease. This is normal and will improve as the interview proceeds. Try to anticipate how you respond when you are nervous and alter your behavior accordingly. Listen carefully to the questions your interviewer asks before you respond. But keep in mind that no matter how much you prepare for interviews, unpredictable questions or situations can arise. This is why I encourage applicants to have an understanding of what they want to convey. At the same time, the unexpected question can really throw the applicant who memorizes and overprepares responses. To keep interviewing interesting for me, every year I prepared one unusual question that I asked all applicants. Inevitably, this question generated some entertaining responses, and I learned unusual things about applicants. I will never forget the applicant whom I asked to teach me something. She got up, saying, "I am going to teach you how to hula hoop." She proceeded to show me the exact way move my hips. This applicant was outstanding, and her colorful response only enhanced my opinion of her since she had a sense of humor, was confident and could spontaneously think outside of the box. If you are asked a question that "throws you," however, **it is perfectly acceptable to pause and say, "Let me think about that." Most people are not comfortable with silences, but they are okay, and your interviewer will always allow you time to think.**

Make sure to close your interview and thank your interviewer

Your interviewer may provide you with an opportunity to make closing remarks, but if he doesn't be sure to make your own opportunity. Close your interview with something strong, sincere, and natural: "I would be honored to matriculate at X for medical school. There is so much about the medical school that I value, and I feel this would be a great fit for me. Thank you so much for taking the time to interview me today." Remember that your interviewer (unless a dean) does not get paid to interview you and volunteers to be on the medical school admissions committee because he or she enjoys meeting applicants and understands the importance of selecting tomorrow's doctors.

CHAPTER 6

HOW SHOULD YOU PREPARE
FOR INTERVIEW DAY?

Review all of your application materials

Anything about which you have written in your application is fair game for discussion. Be sure to review your primary application, secondary application and any update letters you have sent the school. You must be able to speak articulately about each of your experiences, what you learned from them and how they led you to and confirmed your interest in medicine. I strongly discourage applicants from memorizing answers; sounding rehearsed can undermine your authenticity and thus your success. The line between practicing so you are prepared and being over-rehearsed is a fine one. Avoiding sounding "canned" can be especially challenging if you receive multiple interviews and are asked similar questions at all of them.

Be able to speak about any accomplishments or events since you submitted your application

The application process to medical school is fluid, so you can continue to improve your candidacy after you submit your application. Be sure you can speak articulately about what you have done since you submitted your initial application and what you have planned for the year.

Think about your path

The best way to prepare for medical school interviews is to really think about your path and how you got to the seat in which you are sitting on interview day. This may sound simple, but I am always surprised when candidates who obviously have great experiences and have done "all the right things" to get in to medical school cannot connect the dots in their own experience. Think about the overarching themes in your background, when you decided to pursue a career in medicine and what helped confirm your interest. By creating your agenda, you will know your exact path to medicine.

Know the school where you are interviewing

Since medical schools not only want to find the best applicants but also those who are the best fit for their institution, you must know the details about every school where you interview. Review the school's mission statement, philosophy, curriculum, clinical sites where you will be doing rotations, extracurricular and community service opportunities and any recent changes they are promoting. Have an idea of what the school is "known for." For example, is it a research focused institution or does it have a great global or public health program? I also suggest that students review the student profiles that some schools have on their websites to get an idea of the types of people they like (since these profiles will likely be the students of whom they are most proud). Seeking out information may be easy for private schools, but public schools tend to have websites that are more basic and not as informative. For schools that have less than stellar websites, you should seek out information from current students or rely on interview day to become informed about the school.

CHAPTER 7

BEFORE THE INTERVIEW: PRACTICAL CONCERNS

Travel planning

If you are traveling to a different state for your interview, start making your travel arrangements as soon as you set your interview date. This way, if you must travel by air (be sure to carry on your bag), you are likely to get the best fares. Most medical schools have rolling admissions so it is advisable to schedule your interview at the earliest possible date. Some schools are also starting to offer "virtual interviews" or alumni interviews. My advice is to avoid these alternative options until they become more commonplace and only if people become more comfortable with them. Before you make your plans, it also is advisable to contact schools to which you have applied in the same geographic area where you are interviewing. It is perfectly acceptable to call an admissions office and say: "I am interviewing at a medical school close to yours on October 17th and I am trying to economize. I am really interested in your medical school and I was wondering if a decision has been made on my application." Though many students feel this is pushy, as long as you are respectful, this strategy actually has the advantage of communicating that you are a desirable candidate since you have other interviews, probably moving your application to "the top of the pile," and it allows you to express your interest in the school.

It is fine if your parents, significant other or a close friend drives you to the interview since this may alleviate your anxiety, but they should not go to the interview with you. Send them to lunch, perhaps, and tell them you will call them (after you have left the vicinity of the medical complex) once you are finished.

Even if the interview day is supposed to end by 2 PM, do not schedule return flights, trains or rides anytime close to this time. Interviewers may be late and your day may go longer than expected. It is best to make evening travel plans if you are leaving the area the same day as your interview.

Remember that interview season runs from September/October to March/April at most schools so you may well run into winter travel delays. To allow for inclement weather, try not to bunch up interviews too closely together. If you anticipate delays based on a weather prediction, be sure to call the school to let them know about the situation. This communicates that you are reliable and plan ahead.

Sleep
Obviously, you should try to get a good night's sleep the night before your interview. But pre-interview anxiety may make this difficult. For this reason, I advise applicants to get a full eight hours of sleep for the entire week before an interview, making it less likely that one night of sleep deprivation will negatively impact your performance.

Should you stay with a host student?
Many clients ask me about the pros and cons of staying with a host student. A host should not, in theory, have any influence on your candidacy so this concern should not affect your

decision about whether to accept the offer. I suggest doing what will make you most comfortable and help ensure a good night's sleep the night before your interview. For me, staying with a stranger would not be the ideal way to ease anxiety, but this is an individual choice. If you do choose to stay with a host, be respectful; you are a guest in the host's home. In the unlikely event that a host has an influence on your application, keep your conversations a bit more formal than those you would have with a friend; don't say anything negative or tell your host anything you wouldn't want the admissions office to know! If finances are an issue, an alternative would be to stay with a friend or family who lives in the area.

Plan to arrive to your interview at least 15 minutes early

If the school instructs you to arrive for your interview at 9 AM, be there at 8:30 or 8:45 at the latest. Make provisions for rush hour traffic, especially if you are in a city. If you are in a new place, it is also wise to do a "dry run" to the medical school so you know exactly where you are going and how to get there. Academic medical complexes are large and often difficult to navigate. If you are late for any reason, be sure to call the admissions office (you will, of course, have the phone number on hand) and let them know.

Eat breakfast!

Even though some schools may have some pastries or bagels when you arrive, you would be wise to eat a healthy breakfast before your interview, making sure to include some protein and to avoid a high-carbohydrate meal so your blood sugar doesn't plummet while you are interviewing (you will learn more about the pathophysiology of this suggestion during medical school). It is okay to drink some coffee the morning of your interview, but if you are especially anxious consider having only a small cup or skipping the caffeine entirely.

Participate in "optional" activities

Nothing on the interview day agenda should be considered optional. It is essential to demonstrate interest in the school, so opting out of going to classes, for example, communicates that you aren't serious about the school. While such choices do not affect your evaluation, like everything else, your choices send an overall message about you.

Canceling interviews

It is acceptable to cancel interviews, and most schools expect cancelations late in the season. Be sure to call the medical school admissions office at least two weeks before your interview to cancel and send an email to confirm the cancelation. You do not need to give a reason for canceling. No-shows and "night-before" cancelations are unacceptable.

CHAPTER 8

INTERVIEW DAY: THE NITTY GRITTIES

The schedule

Interview days vary but follow a general pattern. Some schools will allow you to go to classes with students, but the schedule generally is similar to the one below.

8:30 AM: Arrive at the interview office
9:00 AM: Presentation by a dean or director of admissions about the school
10:30 AM: Interview #1
12 noon: Lunch
1:00 PM: Interview #2
2:30 PM: School tour conducted by current medical students

What to wear

Consider this your first professional job interview and dress accordingly. By "looking the part," you demonstrate respect for the process, the profession and for the people who are taking time from their day to interview you. If the weather is cold or it is raining, it is fine to wear appropriate gear. You will be given a space to keep your belongings. Above all, I encourage students to be comfortable; while you can't wear your sweatpants, the more comfortable you are, the more confident you will be.

For example, I recently had an applicant who asked me if she should wear her long hair in a bun. When I asked her if she typically wore this hair style, she said, "I have no idea how to put my hair in a bun. A doctor suggested I do this to look more serious." I advised this student to wear her hair as she normally does so she has one less thing to worry about on interview day. If possible, bring an extra blouse/shirt or some stain remover for last minute emergencies.

Women

Medical school applicants sometimes ask me if they can take purses or shoulder bags to interviews. I am always amazed when I read admissions books that suggest women should take only briefcases to interviews or must wear skirts. (see Box 3: What to bring). I think this advice is antiquated and dates back to the 1940s. It is fine to bring a purse, but don't carry your life's possessions with you; smaller is better. Women should wear a pant or skirt suit. The color does not matter as long as the look is professional. Some women wrongly think they must avoid color completely. As long as you are professional, color is okay and can help you stand out from the "sea of navy blue." In fact, I wore a professional red skirt with a more traditionally colored jacket to my medical school interviews. This felt empowering, and boosted my confidence, but these are individual choices. Avoid low cut shirts, short skirts and high heels! Wear conservative jewelry and makeup and comfortable closed-toe shoes (no sandals or open-toe). If you are wearing hose, bring an extra pair.

Most physicians do not wear perfume since patients may have allergies, so it is best to leave scent at home. Polished nails are fine, but the color should be neutral and your nails should be short. Many women who are married ask if they should wear a ring. You should do what makes you comfortable.

Men

Since men have fewer choices, this paragraph is short! It is best to wear a dark suit, but colorful ties are welcome! If you have long hair, consider a cut, and I suggest removing any earrings. It is important to wear comfortable shoes since you will be walking a lot. Be sure to shave before your interview, but leave the aftershave at home. Be neat, tidy and professional.

Remember....

Overall, how you carry yourself typically is more important than what you wear. The person in the high end suit who seems insecure and lacks confidence will not make as good an impression as the individual who shows up in a slightly wrinkled blouse and scuffed shoes, yet is self-assured and exudes enthusiasm and intelligence

Box 3

WHAT TO BRING

I find that many medical school applicants are concerned about what they should bring to interviews.

Do not bring a large backpack to carry around with you

It is too bulky. It's fine to bring a backpack if you must, but plan to ask the admissions office if you can leave it there while you are on your tour and interviews.

It is acceptable to bring a suitcase, if necessary

You can ask where to leave your luggage during your interview. When I interviewed applicants, this situation was commonplace.

Bring a pen and folder or portfolio

You should take notes during program or school presentations, so be prepared. Most programs will give you folders with literature about the school/program. Do not take notes during your actual interview(s).

Bring any recent publications or updates for your interviewers

If you have any recent publications, feel free to bring them to hand to the secretary so they can be added to your file. You can also bring extra copies for your interviewers in case they are interested.

Bring the appropriate outerwear

If you are traveling to a cold climate in the middle of the winter, be prepared. If you wear boots because it is snowing, be sure to bring shoes to which you can change. Similarly, if it is raining, wear appropriate gear. Admissions offices have places to store your belongings.

Bring something to read

Since you will likely have some down time, it is acceptable to bring a book. While I would stay away from romance novels and lightweight magazines, you do not need to bring a medical journal with you. Fiction or the newspaper are fine choices and may even spark some discussion.

Have some cash for incidentals

I will never forget the applicant who asked us for money to buy a sub-
way token. Enough said.

Bring a snack

Just in case you unexpectedly have to wait for your interviewer and you
become hungry, it is wise to have handy something small and incon-
spicuous like a granola bar.

Chapter 9

INTERVIEW ETIQUETTE

Greeting people

Make eye contact with and introduce yourself to everyone you meet and smile naturally! Never call anyone by his first name; use his title and last name. If you aren't sure of the person's title, it is always safe to start off with "Dr. XX." Do not extend your hand when you meet someone; instead let him take this initiative since he is senior to you. Have your right hand free so you are prepared and shake hands firmly if presented with this opportunity. Respect the personal space of everyone you meet. Throughout your interview day, be sure to speak at a normal pace, with clear diction, in a normal tone and volume and in a formal conversational manner. Speaking informally or using slang words anytime during the interview day puts you at risk for being perceived in the wrong way (see Box 4:Interview day tours and lunches: How to behave).

In the office

As you enter someone's office, allow her to suggest where you should sit. If she doesn't, wait for her to sit down first and then sit across from her where it seems most natural. Sit up straight and do not slouch. Place anything you are holding on the floor beside you. If you aren't sure what to do with your hands, fold them comfortably into your lap. It is okay to use gestures while you converse, but don't go overboard. Do not forget to smile and try to appear positive, energetic, enthusiastic and warm. Be sure to make eye contact with your interviewer throughout the interview, especially when she is talking. This demonstrates that you are attentive. This behavior will make your interviewer like you—a primary goal. Do not be offended if your interviewer's pager or cell phone goes off and she needs to answer a call. This is medicine and things come up.

Closing the interview

When it is obvious that your interview is over, allow your interviewer to stand up first and then you stand up and grab any belongings. Allow your interviewer to continue to the door first and then follow him. He will likely say something like, "I enjoyed meeting you. Do you know how to get to where you need to go?" You should respond: "Thank you for your time. I would be thrilled to come here for medical school and, yes, I know where I am going." Since your interviewer now feels acquainted with you personally, he may give you a mentor-like "pat" or extend his hand for a handshake. Again, pay attention and follow your interviewer's lead.

Following up after the interview

Write thank you notes or emails. They are unlikely to influence your candidacy, but it is good manners to write these notes. Make the note short and sweet and mention anything that was a highlight of your interview; also repeat that you are interested in the school and thank the interviewer for her time. Sometimes admissions offices give applicants suggestions for contacting their interviewers so, if they do, be sure to follow their directions. But wait until you get home to send your thank you notes. I remember the candidate who was writing her thank you notes in the conference room during interview day. She handed them to the secretary before she left. This seemed contrived and insincere.

Box 4

INTERVIEW DAY TOURS AND LUNCHES: HOW TO BEHAVE

General

Many clients ask me about how to behave on tours and lunches during interview days. The bottom line is: Always be respectful.

Whether you are interacting with a secretary, admissions director or the person who takes away the trash, it is essential to treat everyone well. Making a strong impression can help you if that impression is positive or hurt you if it is negative. How you treat the support staff is crucial; it says a lot about your character, and even a hint of entitlement or rudeness can significantly hinder your success.

Also be kind to other applicants. Pretend you are in a fishbowl during your medical school interview day. If you are friendly and personable to all, it can only help your candidacy and affect the overall impression that people have of you.

Be sure to turn off your cell phone, and do not check email during your interview day. You must appear attentive and undistracted the entire day.

Tours

On tours, be front and center, pay attention and make eye contact to demonstrate that you are paying attention. When I was a tour guide, I could always tell who was lingering, chatting or was disinterested and who was really paying attention to what I said. While it is good to ask questions, don't dominate or interrupt the tour guide.

Be kind to other applicants

Pretend you are in a fishbowl during your medical school interview day and constantly being observed. If you are friendly and personable to all, it can only help your candidacy and favorably affect the overall impression that people have of you. Don't spend your time talking about other schools and comparing notes.

Lunch

Avoid caffeinated beverages during lunch if you are nervous. Demonstrate good table manners. Also, never chew gum, though it is okay to bring breath mints with you. Do not eat a large lunch if your interviews follow the meal as this may make you sleepy.

Don't...ever...

Talk negatively about another medical school, applicant or your undergraduate school.

CHAPTER 10

WHAT HAPPENS AFTER YOU LEAVE?

The written summary

Typically, interviewers fill out a written summary of your candidacy. They "grade" you on your accomplishments, academics, research, letters of reference, and ability to overcome adversity, among other factors in your candidacy. They also grade you on your personality, enthusiasm, ability to communicate, empathy, compassion, leadership ability and motivation for a career in medicine. They try to determine if they believe you will do well as a medical student, contribute to the medical community and would be a good fit for the school. Interviewers may fill this form out immediately after your interview or sometime during the day when they have time. They will likely refer to their notes and your application when completing this form, but how they evaluate you will mostly be based on their overall impression of you. Sometimes, these forms are submitted to the senior members of the admissions committee, who make a decision about your acceptance, rejection or wait list status, but more often your interviewer "presents" you at a meeting of all members of the admission committee.

The verbal summary

Admissions committee meetings are usually held weekly so, for example, if meetings are on Mondays and your interviews were on a Tuesday, your interviewers will each "present you" based on what they have written and on what they remember the following week. The "snapshot" that your interviewers present typically takes no more than five minutes, and they tell the other members of the committee what they suggest should be the decision on your application. Then, all members vote on your candidacy, and the outcome of the vote usually seals the decision. So, you can see that if your interviewers advocate for you, they essentially make the decision about your fate. It does happen that two interviewers disagree about a candidate, and this is when things get interesting. It is also why it is so important to have an interviewer who will really go to bat for you and fight for your candidacy. Some admissions committees allow vetoes, so if a member strongly feels that a candidate should be rejected, this decision cannot be overturned. Ultimately, the dean of admissions makes all decisions and theoretically can overturn a committee decision, but this almost never happens unless some vital piece of information is uncovered after an interview.

What is a typical "committee presentation"?

"Applicant X is an outstanding young man. He grew up in California and was initially inspired to pursue a career in medicine when his grandfather became ill. He has volunteered in hospitals since high school and has done in depth research. He also is committed to helping the underserved and has volunteered in a free clinic for four years. He graduated from college in May and is spending this year doing oncology research and is likely to be published. He has extensive shadowing, volunteer and leadership experiences. He did poorly his freshman year with an overall GPA of 3.0 because he was adjusting to college, but he rebounded his sophomore through senior years with a 3.6 – 3.8 average. He has a 33 on his MCAT with an even distribution. His letters of reference are outstanding and support my assessment of him. This young man is sensitive, compassionate, humble, intellectually curious and is clearly motivated to become a physician scientist. I think he would be a wonderful fit here and he seems sincere that he would like to attend. I think we should take him."

Surprisingly, most committee presentations are brief and boil down your candidacy to a nutshell. And, assuming that all interviewers agree, these committee votes and decisions can be quick!

CHAPTER 11

THE BA/MD INTERVIEW

Accelerated (6- or 7-year) medical programs are designed for high school students who know they want to pursue careers in medicine. Often, these programs involve two sets of interviews; one is with the undergraduate college and one is with the medical school. Most accelerated programs require students to maintain a certain grade point average in their undergraduate course work to keep their position in the medical school. Every year I receive calls from students who were unable to meet this criterion. Typically, students fail to maintain the minimum GPA because they become distracted by social activities, take their medical school seat for granted or find other interests when they have freedom and are somewhat removed from parental pressure.

Thus, interviewers at these programs are trying to assess several characteristics:
1) Are you mature?
2) Are you truly committed to a career in medicine, and do you understand what it means to be a physician?
3) Are you going to "make it?"

Your interviewer wants to be sure that you have the diligence, focus, maturity and discipline to take on a rigorous course load. They also want to know that you are pursuing this path because it is what you want and not because of pressure from your parents. Your interviewer is trying to assess the likelihood that you will succeed if you don't have your parents around to "keep you on track." The path you are taking will not be easy and will require you to work incredibly hard and interviewers need to make sure you realize this.

What are some interview questions that are unique to BS/MD programs?

1) What will be the greatest challenges you will face in this program?
2) Why do you want to pursue an accelerated program rather than the traditional route to medical school?
3) How do you know you want to be a doctor?
4) What have you done without the influence of your parents?
5) How do you manage your time and remember everything you need to do?
6) What undergraduate studies interest you?

CHAPTER 12

THE CARIBBEAN MEDICAL SCHOOL INTERVIEW

Caribbean medical school interviews take place in the United States either at a school's US home office or with a graduate of the school. If the interview is conducted at a school office, an administrator typically conducts it. Alumni interviewers may be residents or practicing physicians. Alumni interviewers do not get paid; they are volunteers. Caribbean medical school interviews are usually fairly low stress and consist of basic interview questions. Interviewers are trying to assess your interest in their specific school and want to know that you will be able to cope while studying on a Caribbean island where you will be far away from home and won't have the luxuries to which you may be accustomed. Many people say living on a Caribbean island is often similar to living in a third world country so your interviewer wants to know that you will be able to handle this situation. That said, since Caribbean medical schools are "for profit" and may not have the same limited enrollments as US schools, many interviewers are not overly concerned with these issues since they aren't sacrificing a seat in the class if you "don't make it."

What are some specific questions you may be asked on these interviews?

1) Why do you want to go to school in the Caribbean?
2) What are your expectations of going to school in the Caribbean?
3) What are some of the challenges you anticipate by going to school here?
4) How will you cope with being so far away from your family?

At least one major Caribbean medical school asks applicants to write a short essay during the interview, but this is reputed to be a low stress, easy exercise that evaluates your ability to communicate.

APPENDIX A

THE SAMPLE INTERVIEW

Create an outline for your answers to the following questions, which are certainly going to be asked at most, if not all, of your interviews:

Tell me about yourself.
This is what I call a launching pad question, which can come in other versions, such as "What brings you here today?" or "Tell me why you are here." This question presents an opportunity to paint a picture of yourself and present all of the information you hope to discuss in your interview. While you don't want to go into too much detail about any one activity or experience in your response, you do want to give your interviewer enough material so she can ask more questions about the topics you mention. Questions like this one are ice breakers and give you the opportunity to really control an interview and set the stage for what will be discussed.

A sample answer:
I am 26 years old and currently am working in oncology research. I grew up in Southern California with my parents, who emigrated from Russia. My grandparents also lived with us and we had

a tightly knit family. I have been interested in medicine since my grandfather became sick when I was a freshman in high school. I had just started high school biology, and I often went with him to his doctor's appointments and helped him at home. I became curious about the drugs he was taking and what was going on with his body. I also was concerned about his emotional state and appreciated the vital role his doctor played in helping him cope with his illness. I have been volunteering in hospitals since that time. During high school I was also on the debate team and played varsity tennis. I enrolled in college and had a tough time my freshman year since I was not prepared for the more rigorous academic environment. But I improved my study skills and did better in subsequent years. I majored in biology with a minor in anthropology. I also gained extensive exposure to a variety of specialties through shadowing. After my junior year of college, I started working in the lab where I now work during the summer, and I have enjoyed my research so much that I decided to take this year to dedicate myself to it. Throughout college I also volunteered at a middle school tutoring underserved children and was heavily involved in the student government. Through my involvement in a nearby free clinic where I still volunteer I also gained a greater understanding of the challenges facing many US citizens. I have been looking forward to this day for a long time, and I was hoping to get an interview here and I thank you for inviting me.

Why this is a good answer:

The applicant creates a clear picture of himself, his motivations and his path, along with his low grades his freshman year – a possible "red flag." Now his interviewer can "cherry pick" what he would like to discuss, including:

1) His background
2) What most impacted the applicant about his grandfather's care

3) His research experience
4) His low grades freshman year
4) His shadowing experiences
5) His tutoring experiences
6) His academics
7) His involvement in student government
8) His involvement in a free clinic

Why do you want to be a doctor?

I am always a bit surprised when I ask this question, and the student fails to mention anything about patient care. Be sure to mention helping patients as the cornerstone of your motivations to pursue a career in medicine. I encourage most clients to answer this question both in terms of "when" and "why." This enables you to tell the interviewer about your longstanding (ideally) motivation to pursue a career in medicine. You can also use segues to bring up various medically related experiences and your future career plans, which will provide your interviewer with more material to ask about.

Sample answer:

Well, as I mentioned when we started talking, my interest in medicine really began when my grandfather was sick. He had heart disease and I was so intrigued by what was going on with his body and how his medications helped treat his illnesses. I was also inspired by the doctors who treated him and in particular by his cardiologist who was compassionate and really seemed to care about my grandfather and our family. Not only was this doctor technically competent and knowledgeable, but he also treated my grandfather as he would treat his own father. I could see that many physicians treated my grandfather differently because he was an immigrant and did not speak English well. But his cardiologist didn't do this, and I was determined to be like him – able to care for patients sensitively while being intellectually challenged and utilizing technical skills. Since then I have learned about research, and I now understand that in medicine I can combine a career in clinical medicine and research, which is what I hope to do in the future. I also hope to volunteer as a physician, probably domestically, because my work at the free clinic has shown me a need to help those who do not have access to care. I want to be a doctor to make a valuable contribution to people's health and well-being while making a more far-reaching impact through research.

Why this is a good answer:

1) Student provides background to demonstrate the duration of his interest

2) He demonstrates compassion, empathy and cultural competence

3) He shows that he understands what it means to practice medicine

4) He implies that he is intellectually curious

5) He gives an idea of his future plans, which incorporate all of his past experiences and thus he seems directed and committed to a career in medicine

6) He demonstrates his understanding of others and issues related to our health system by mentioning his free clinic work

7) He provides segues and prompts for the interviewer to ask more questions

Why our school?

Medical schools are looking for the best candidates but they are also seeking students who are the best fit for their school. It is essential that you research the school where you are interviewing and have specific reasons why you want to attend. Avoid "telling them what they want to hear" and choose things that are aligned with your demonstrated interests. For example, if you are an avid researcher with five original publications, do not be offended if a school focusing on primary care does not offer you an acceptance even if their average "stats" are lower than yours. You must convince the interviewer that you would be a good fit for the school and that you can best achieve your goals and ideals at that specific school.

Sample answer:

I want to go to your medical school for many reasons. First of all, the school has early clinical exposure, which I think is important and fosters an environment of collaboration through the use of small groups and problem based learning. I also appreciate the school's curriculum and the block system. I value that the student and patient populations are diverse, which is also important to me. I enjoy working with people who are different than I and learning about them, which is one of the reasons I enjoyed tutoring underserved children. If I were to become a student here I would do research, and the school is a leader in my field of research. I think that I would find many role models here who could help mentor me to become a physician scientist, and the educational environment would be stimulating. I am also interested in learning more about the impact of culture on how people perceive health care and there is an elective focused specifically on this topic, which I would pursue. And, I would join the student run clinic because this is work that I currently value now at the free clinic where I volunteer. I would also be thrilled to move to this city and experience a new part of the country.

Why this is a good answer:

1) Student shows he is knowledgeable and informed about the school

2) He identifies specific reasons why he is interested in the school

3) He presents himself as an ideal fit for the school by identifying some of his own values that mirror the school's philosophy and mission

4) He mentions his own interest in research, which likely distinguishes him from other applicants and how he envisions making a contribution to the school

5) He also mentions his tutoring and free clinic work, providing a prompt for his interviewer

APPENDIX B

OTHER POPULAR QUESTIONS

Tell me about a challenging time in your life.

The interviewer may ask about a time when you weren't successful or about your greatest failure. "I can't think of anything" is the wrong answer. This response demonstrates lack of insight; we have all had challenges. The interviewer wants to know that you can cope with adversity and how you do it and that you learn from challenging times. He also wants to know that you are resilient and resourceful.

Sample answer:

A challenging time for me was when I started college. I had always done very well in high school, and I didn't expect that I would find college so difficult both academically and socially. It was the first time I lived away from my family, and I was homesick. I also found the work load heavier than in high school, and good grades did not come as easily. I learned to manage my time better and improved my study habits. But I also made a real effort to make new friends and adapt to my new environment. In retrospect, I realize that stepping out of my comfort zone was one of the best choices I ever made. This forced me to grow, mature and adapt, and the skills I gained will help me in the future. I now understand that challenging myself helps me to grow in many ways.

Why this is a good answer:
1) The student is honest and authentic
2) He presents the challenge and the solutions
3) He conveys that he can persevere
4) He conveys that he learned from this experience
5) He makes it clear that he understands that such situations are likely to occur again and that he is better equipped to cope with them

What would you say is one of the major problems with our health care system today?

As I have mentioned, no one expects you to be an expert in health policy. If asked this question (and many interviewers don't even touch on this topic because it is so complex), you want to convey that you have an overall understanding of the issues and that you understand that they are complicated. I suggest that applicants read about health care reform during their application year at least once a week so they feel better prepared to discuss these issues, but my impression is that few interviewees are asked in detail about health care reform.

Sample answer:
Wow. The issues of health care reform are so complex, and I am trying to grasp them. I think one of the biggest concerns is lack of access to care for the uninsured. For example, at the free clinic where I work, many patients present with complications of disease and we must then refer them to the emergency department for further care. This is because they do not have access to primary providers and because they often do not take their medications or care for themselves. I think if we increased awareness of prevention for

underserved communities and made it easier somehow for them to live healthier lifestyles and increased their access to care by providing them with some kind of coverage, we would decrease our health care spending because these actions would help prevent disease.

Why this is a good answer:

1) The interviewee admits he has a lot to learn
2) He then goes on to explain some of the issues with access to care, patient education and patient compliance
3) He also demonstrates cultural competence by recognizing that achieving a healthy lifestyle is not easy for certain populations
4) He suggests some solutions to these problems
5) He mentions his firsthand experience caring for the underserved

Do you have any questions for me?

Most students feel they must have questions to ask at the close of an interview, but unless you have an interviewer whom you sense wants you to ask a question, it is not always necessary to do so. Realize that not everyone agrees with me on this point, and some people advise applicants always to ask questions, regardless of the circumstances. But I feel this is disingenuous, and I could always tell when applicants asked questions because they thought it was the right thing to do. Not only was this a waste of time for both of us, but it sometimes diluted positive feelings I had about the interview before then.

The applicant must also pay attention to an interviewer's cues, however. For example, if an interviewer says, "So, **what** questions do you have for me?" it implies that you should have some. (If your interviewer is an "egomaniac" or a "talker," he likely will want you to ask questions.) But if she asks, "Do you have **any** questions?" coming up with something is not obligatory. A good strategy is to ask questions during your interview, assuming it has a conversational tone. This has the advantage of seeming more natural and sincere and allows you, when asked about any additional queries at the end of the interview, to answer truthfully, "You have already answered all my questions."

If you feel you must ask questions, you should try to ask questions that relate to your interests and demonstrate your interest in and knowledge of the school. It is also safe to ask about how much elective time students receive to pursue their interests in other specialties, if the school has a formal mentorship program, if students receive guidance when it is time to apply to residency or, if you have a specific interest, you can ask about opportunities in that area. Don't ask questions that you could easily find out the answers to on the school's website.

Sample answer #1:

I don't have any specific questions. I have studied every page of the school's website because I am so interested in this school. The presentation and tour today were also very thorough, so I feel that all of my questions have been answered. I would be really happy to attend medical school here and think it would be a great fit for me. If I think of any additional questions after I leave, to whom should I address these? Thanks for everything.

Why this is a good answer:

1) It communicates to the interviewer that he prepared for the interview
2) It communicates to the interviewer that he is informed about the school
3) It demonstrates honesty and authenticity
4) It transforms the question into a statement about his enthusiasm for the school
5) By making this transformation the interviewer forgets what he asked the applicant in the first place
6) It expresses gratitude for being considered and interviewed

Sample answer #2:

Most of my questions have been addressed today, and I must say that I think this school is the perfect fit for me. But, I was wondering how many students actually work at the student run free clinic and if there might be opportunities for me to take on a significant role there since I am interested in working there.

Why this is a good answer:

1) The student communicates that he is prepared
2) The student expresses his interest in the school
3) The student asks about something that is related to his interest.
4) The student demonstrates that he plans on taking on a significant role outside of the classroom while a medical student.

What is your greatest weakness?

Personally, I can't stand this question and never asked it. I find that it is typically the unskilled interviewer who poses this question, but medical school applicants are always nervous about fielding this question. Most often, applicants are advised to choose a strength that is actually a weakness, such as "I am a perfectionist." "I have a tough time saying no to opportunities." "I sometimes work so hard that I sacrifice my free time." I suggest simply being sincere. Give a real, honest answer but not one that would be a deal breaker for medical school, such as "I can't work on teams."

Sample answer:

I tend to procrastinate. I am constantly trying to improve this weakness because my procrastination causes me a lot of stress. And, when I get stressed because I am close to a deadline or exam, I am not very pleasant to be around. But, this stress is also what motivates me to get the job done.

Why this is a good answer:
1) This applicant cites a real weakness
2) He gives it a positive "spin"
3) He appears authentic and genuine

A 16-year-old girl comes to your office with her mother. As you do routinely, you ask the mother to leave so you can talk to the girl openly. The patient confides in you that she is sexually active and asks you to prescribe birth control pills, but she does not want her mother to know. What do you do?

Ethical and "behavioral" questions can be tough. The "right" answers are not always obvious, and the key is to consider all aspects of the described situation and to consider what is in the best interest of the patient. The interviewer is looking for your "answer," of course, but he is also interested in your thought process, reasoning, ability to verbalize and to identify the issues and be sensitive to them, and whether you communicate that you are compassionate and considerate. Typically these types of questions are also designed to evaluate your professionalism, ability to work as a member of a team, values, ethics and cultural competence.

Sample answer:

This is a tough question. First of all, I would educate the patient about the risk of unprotected sex with regard to sexually transmitted diseases and HIV. I would let her know that pregnancy was not the only consideration. I would also make sure she was sexually active because she wanted to be and that she was in no way being pressured. I would then ask what she was using for birth control. I would tell her that her mother should be aware that she is sexually active and of the risks of taking birth control pills and strongly advise her to take her mother into her confidence. However, I would offer this advice within the context of an assessment of the relationship she has with her mother. Ultimately, I don't know if I would prescribe the pills because it would depend on that state's laws regarding treating a minor, but I would want to protect this girl and wouldn't want her to become pregnant because I didn't prescribe her the medication. At the same time, I wouldn't want to encourage her sexual activity by giving her the prescription. I think I would seek out help from a social worker and would make sure to schedule a follow-up appointment with this patient once I had time to consider the legal issues and to learn more about other issues in her life and her family situation.

Why this is a good answer:

1) The applicant considers this situation from multiple perspectives

2) He considers how his actions will impact not only the patient but her family and the individual with whom she is having a sexual relationship

3) He demonstrates that he thinks clearly and objectively

4) He admits that he doesn't know the applicable laws but is aware that they vary by state

5) He demonstrates compassion, empathy, professionalism and an understanding of the complexities of the situation

6) He demonstrates resourcefulness and his ability to consider the other members of his "team"

APPENDIX C

OTHER TOPICS AND QUESTIONS YOU MAY BE ASKED

I do not pose answers to the following potpourri of questions or topics you may be asked to address because I strongly discourage applicants from simply telling interviewers what they think they want to hear. How you deal with the following will depend on your background and experiences; demonstrating authenticity, honesty and consistency are key, so should any of these questions or subjects come up, address them in a fashion that is consistent with your application, experience and letters of reference.

If you had a free day what would you do?

How do you achieve balance in your life?

Tell me a joke.

Teach me something.

What experience(s) made you want to pursue medicine?

How would your best friend describe you? What would he or she say is your greatest weakness?

What activity have you pursued on your own without the influence of your parents?

What is something you tried really hard at but didn't turn out as expected or what has been your greatest challenge?

Did you ever have to work to help support yourself or fund your education?

How do you remember everything you have to do?

How will you deal with debt?

Where have you traveled around the world?

Would you change anything in your background? What and why?

What would you do if you could not pursue a career in medicine?

Tell me about your research/clinical work/volunteer experience.

Explain your academic path.

What strengths would you bring to the medical school?

Why did you do a special master's program/MBA etc.?

Explain your poor grade/MCAT/academic performance.

How would you add to the diversity of our school?

Tell me about an ethical dilemma and how you decided what to do.

What qualities should a physician possess?

What qualities do you possess that will help you to become a physician?

Tell me about the most influential person in your life.

Tell me about your most valued mentor.

What is your most valuable accomplishment?

What direct clinical exposure do you have?

What leadership roles have you held?

Why should we choose you?

What should I tell the admissions committee about you?

Describe your perfect day.

Where do you see yourself in the future (10, 20 or 30 years)?

If you could change anything about your education, what would that be and why?

What kinds of books do you read? Tell me about the book you read most recently.

What do you do for fun?

In closing, is there anything else you would like to tell me?

What have you done since you graduated from college?

APPENDIX D

QUESTIONS TO ASK YOUR INTERVIEWER

The best questions to ask interviewers are related specifically to the applicant's interests and background. Below are some basic questions you can ask your faculty interviewer.

General

How would you describe a typical medical student here?

What are the most positive aspects of this school?

How do you like being on faculty here?

What do you do/what is your specialty?

Curriculum

Do you anticipate any upcoming changes to the curriculum?

Can I access lectures via the web or on line?

Do students typically do research for credit?

What do most students do during their first year summer?

Are there global health opportunites?

What are the options for fourth year elective rotations?

Mentoring
Is there a formal guidance program here?

Do students receive help when applying for residency?

Are clinical faculty supportive of students?

Rotations
Do students have bedside teaching on rotations?

Are rotations crowded; do students compete for patients, procedures or teaching?

Where do students complete most clinical rotations?

After medical school
What are the most popular specialties that students pursue?

What percentage of students complete residencies at hospitals affilitated with the medical school?

APPENDIX E

QUESTIONS TO ASK THE CURRENT MEDICAL STUDENTS

General

Are you happy?

Why did you choose to come here?

What are the best things about the school?

Do you think that what was presented to you on interview day was accurate?

How do you like living here?

Curriculum

What are the strengths and weakness of the curriculum?

Do you know of any changes in the curriculum?

Are faculty supportive of student feedback regarding the curriculum?

Clinical Rotations

What do you think of the clinical sites?

Is there bedside teaching?

Is most teaching done by housestaff or faculty?

What are the best/worst rotations here?

Are you learning how to practice evidenced based medicine?

Do you think you have enough flexibility to choose elective rotations?

Research

Do most students do research?

Do you have to seek out opportunities on your own?

Teaching and mentoring

Do faculty and residents teach?

Do you have enough 1:1 time with residents and faculty?

Do faculty help with specialty selection and the match process?

Student Life

How would you describe the comaraderie between students?

What do students do in their free time?

Where do students live?

How do most students get to school?

Do students participate in volunteer, community service or teaching activities?

APPENDIX F

A SAMPLE THANK YOU NOTE

Thank you notes to your interviewers will not influence your candidacy but it is good manners to write them. Ideally, your notes should be concise yet should touch on some aspect of your interview that was unique. You should also mention something that you like about the school that relates to your interests and the topics discussed during your interview. Just like other aspects of this process, your note should reflect the tone of your interview. For example, if you had a great connection with an interviewer, your note might be longer and more personal. But, if your interview was brief and superficial, you might only mention specific things you like about the school.

Dear Dr. XXX,

Thank you very much for taking the time to interview me on November 5th. I really enjoyed meeting you and learning about Academic Medical School. I think that Academic would be a great fit for me. I appreciate the new integrated curriculum and feel that this suits my learning style. I am also intrigued by the opportunity to work at the student run clinic which would allow me to continue helping the underserved. I hope your lecture at the National Society of Esteemed Faculty went well.

I would be honored to learn from you as a student at Academic. If there is any thing else you need to evaluate my candidacy, please let me now.

Best regards,

Prospective Student

What does this student do?

1. Thanks the interviewer for his time

2. Mentions the new curriculum

3. Mentions his interest in the underserved

4. Brings up something that was discussed at the interview

5. Offers to provide additional information

Personalized practice mock interview sessions with a knowledgeable professional who has served on a medical school admissions committee is the best way to prepare for medical school interviews. Dr. Jessica Freedman offers comprehensive assistance with all aspects of the medical school admissions process.

For more information on the services offered by MedEdits, feel free to contact us.

Visit our website: www.MedEdits.com

Read Dr. Freedman's blog: www.MedEdits.blogspot.com

Call 201.244.6142

Email: info@mededits.com.

We would also value feedback on this book so we can modify future editions.

What MedEdits' clients are saying about Dr. Freedman:

"I think what we talked about regarding interviews made a huge difference-I had a very cohesive story to tell and was better prepared for the last two interviews-I wish I had known about you sooner before I had my earlier interviews! I felt as if God had sent you to us. Again, my deepest thanks". {Follow up: Applicant matriculated at their first choice school where they interviewed after prepping with Dr. Freedman.}

"Dr. Freedman has been wonderfully helpful and supportive throughout the AMCAS process. Dr. Freedman did do a lot for not only me this year, but also my family (sisters, parents and grandparents) who have been watching me struggle with medical school applications these last two years. Her aim is find out what drives a pre-medical student to become a future physician, and single out qualities that make an applicant unique. I received help with editing my activities section and personal statement, as well as practiced interviewing with Dr. Freedman. Her help allowed me to express my passion for the field and to better articulate the strength of my application. More importantly, she helped me realize that I was an asset to the field. After being rejected two times from medical schools, despite a good GPA and solid MCAT scores, I felt that there was something inherently wrong with me. After picking apart my application, Dr. Freedman pointed out where and why schools were overlooking my application... Mock interviews with Dr. Freedman gave me confidence to approach interviews with an attitude of eagerness to learn rather than a self-contained, reticent disposition. I will be entering an excellent medical school next year, and my gratitude to Dr. Freedman and MedEdits for their help is endless. I recommend her services to anyone who is eager to pursue medicine with a drive to help better the healthcare field, and the quality of patient care."

"Before speaking with Dr. Freedman, I was under the assumption that the application process itself did not matter and that my work and scores would speak for themselves. This was not the case and sadly I learned the hard way when I was rejected by all medical schools my first round. Then, I hired Dr. Freedman. After using Dr. Freedman's services to prepare for my first interview during my second round of applying, I realized how important it was to unveil and highlight my best qualities. The application process is critical as it is your opportunity to show who you are. Dr. Freedman convinced me of this and helped me to perfect my self-presentation. Throughout the application process, she was always available, flexible and responsive to every query. Furthermore, I always feel at ease in our conversations and absolutely trust every piece of advice she offers. She is never wrong! I ended up getting into my first choice school and am thrilled with the results of her counseling. I definitely intend to use Dr. Freedman's assistance for my residency process. Thank you again, Dr. Freedman!"

"I GOT INTO MEDICAL SCHOOL!!! Thank you so much. I cannot tell you how much it has meant to have your support, Dr. Freedman. Looking back on this process, there was no one that offered better advice or preparation for my essays and the interview. It was such a great advantage to have your insider's knowledge of the admission system and without a doubt it helped me greatly... I have already told all of my friends about Dr. Freedman. But, I can honestly say that without D. Freedman's help I do not think I would have had half the success I had. There are a millions of nuances involved with medical school admissions. Dr. Freedman has the valuable experience and she will truly dedicate herself to your application... The admission process is very long and challenging. By having Dr. Freedman on my side I had an advisor focused on my application. She provided detailed help at every stage of the process. Working with Dr. Freedman made me certain that I was doing everything I could to get into medical school. She has hundreds of tips from her years working in admissions that really make the difference"

Made in the USA
Lexington, KY
26 August 2012